#MRNotes

Volume 1: August 4, 2015 –
April 29, 2019

T.S. Lim
May 7, 2019

#MRNotes by T.S. Lim is licensed under a Creative Commons Attribution-Non Commercial 4.0 International License, except where otherwise noted.

Table of Contents

Preface 3
2015 4
    August 2015 4
    September 2015 4
    October 2015 5
    November 2015 5
    December 2015 6
2016 7
    January 2016 7
    February 2016 7
    March 2016 7
    April 2016 8
    May 2016 8
    June 2016 9
    July 2016 9
    August 2016 10
    September 2016 10
    October 2016 11
    November 2016 11
    December 2016 12
2017 13
    January 2017 13
    February 2017 13
    March 2017 14
    April 2017 14
    May 2017 14
    June 2017 15
    July 2017 15
    August 2017 16
    September 2017 16
    October 2017 16
    November 2017 17

    December 2017 17
2018 19
    January 2018 19
    February 2018 19
    March 2018 20
    April 2018 20
    May 2018 21
    June 2018 21
    July 2018 22
    August 2018 22
    September 2018 23
    October 2018 23
    November 2018 24
    December 2018 25
2019 26
    January 2019 26
    February 2019 26
    March 2019 27
    April 2019 27
About the Author 29

Preface

Dear Readers:

#MRNotes is a collection of my personal opinion. The notes have been based on my direct observations in the real world, from my interactions with clients, prospects, or colleagues, from reading offline and online news, from doing many actual marketing research projects, from reading books and papers, from the mistakes that I have made, and from my own reflection.

In Volume 1, there are 191 notes spanning from August 4, 2015, when I published #MRNotes for the first time, till April 29, 2019.

I publish the note on my LinkedIn page (https://www.linkedin.com/in/tslim/) weekly on every Monday. The exception was the note I published too soon on Sunday January 1, 2017.

The note is also forwarded automatically to my Twitter (https://twitter.com/tslim) and Facebook (https://www.facebook.com/tslim1) accounts. Unfortunately, I forgot to click the option to forward it automatically to Twitter and Facebook on four dates. Since LinkedIn keeps posts for only a year, there are then four missing entries in Volume 1 of #MRNotes. The missing entries are from the following dates:

- January 18, 2016
- September 18, 2017
- September 25, 2017
- December 18, 2017

I hope you enjoy reading the notes and can avoid making the same mistakes that I did in the past.

Warm regards,
T.S. Lim
ts.lim@leap-research
Quantitative Senior Research Director & Partner
Leap Research

May 7, 2019
Jakarta, Indonesia

2015

August 2015

Volume forecast follows a branded test like a concept test or a concept-product test, and not an unbranded one. (4-Aug-15)

Sample size determination is in the end a function of research budget or stimulus availability. (10-Aug-15)

Marketing research can help business owners to identify potential consumers. (18-Aug-15)

Before adopting a cheaper ingredient in a product, test it among the loyal users to avoid alienation. (24-Aug-15)

Research design determines the analytics that can be applied, and vice versa. (31-Aug-15)

September 2015

A good branded evaluation should take into account the competition. (8-Sep-15)

Volume forecast in the FMCG world requires that we talk to all potential buyers to obtain the most accurate number. (14-Sep-15)

It's expected that branded and unbranded product tests may yield different results. (21-Sep-15)

Performance of a recently launched product should always be evaluated via a post launch check survey. (28-Sep-15)

October 2015

Testing a new product branded but unpriced is dangerous since in the end price does matter. (5-Oct-15)

Respondents' fatigue must be taken into account seriously when designing a questionnaire. (12-Oct-15)

If an initiative is important enough, then there should be a proper written research brief. (19-Oct-15)

It's a bad practice to cover many different topics in one research project. (26-Oct-15)

November 2015

Unless the questionnaire is very simple and short, interviewing by street intercept is to be avoided. (2-Nov-15)

If a particular brand image is problematic within an organization, then it'd be better to exclude in from the survey questionnaire. (9-Nov-15)

Before discussing sample size requirement, check first the size of the universe population. (16-Nov-15)

Avoid asking two questions with highly correlated answers. (23-Nov-15)

It's futile to ask respondents what they want directly in a marketing research project. (30-Nov-15)

December 2015

Marketing research can help business owners to understand their current consumers. (7-Dec-15)

The validity of the result of a marketing research project depends on the unbiased research design, not on the size of the sample. (14-Dec-15)

Users of marketing research services must acknowledge that each analytical solution has its own limitation. (21-Dec-15)

Sampling theory makes it possible for us not to collect data from every location / area. (28-Dec-15)

2016

January 2016

Statistics can help in providing guidance to assess if the observed difference between two scores really matters. (4-Jan-16)

The availability of DIY survey platform doesn't guarantee good questionnaires. (11-Jan-16)

Procuring market research services is not the same as procuring tangible goods. (25-Jan-16)

February 2016

A quality research proposal can be written if clients can provide agencies with a quality research brief. (1-Feb-16)

Research is valuable if it can be translated into tangible marketing actions (in Steven A. Silbiger. The Ten-Day MBA 4th Ed. 2012). (8-Feb-16)

Questionnaire design & writing are both science & art. (15-Feb-16)

Randomness shouldn't be a determining factor when deciding to conduct mobile surveys. (22-Feb-16)

Marketeers must master the market research principles to be able to collaborate well with MR agencies to solve business issues. (29-Feb-16)

March 2016

The number of questions in a mobile survey via a smartphone must be really limited to get good quality data. (7-Mar-16)

Survey length should be determined by the number of questions asked, not the length of interview. (14-Mar-16)

You must not use marketing research to try to elicit confidential information from respondents. (21-Mar-16)

If you can't accept the findings, then you'd better not conduct any marketing research in the first place. (28-Mar-16)

April 2016

There are only two informative open-end questions in product testing projects; i.e., spontaneous likes and dislikes. (4-Apr-16)

Data collection method depends on the research objectives, analytics, cost & time constraints, and country specific limitation. (11-Apr-16)

You must have a clear definition for every possible answers in each question in your questionnaire. (18-Apr-16)

Members of Consumer Insight Department should master Marketing Research principles to collaborate well with research agencies. (25-Apr-16)

May 2016

Creating a rate card is a futile exercise if the project specifications are vague. (2-May-16)

A well executed segmentation exercise will depend heavily on pre-determined crystal clear business objectives. (9-May-16)

Asking too detailed purchase habit in a survey is really problematic since memory fades very quickly. (16-May-16)

A new product launch shouldn't be left to an inexperienced brand team with only a limited knowledge about marketing research. (23-May-16)

Business objectives in a marketing research project must come from the brand team. (30-May-16)

June 2016

All specific research questions must be specified by all stakeholders before embarking on a marketing research project. (6-Jun-16)

Pricing research is intended to answer some very specific research questions in a simulated environment. (13-Jun-16)

In this digital age, marketing research is still all about excellent operations. (20-Jun-16)

You need to put yourself in your respondent's shoes when asking him/her to fill in a diary you've created. (27-Jun-16)

July 2016

Manipulating fixed format ASCII data is a dying skill in marketing research. (4-Jul-16)

It's more important to reach the right target respondents than to be fast. (11-Jul-16)

The proposal writer(s) must get involved in executing the project to ensure common sense is upheld in designing the study. (18-Jul-16)

It shouldn't come as a surprise to see a difference in awareness level when comparing two tracking waves with a one year gap. (25-Jul-16)

August 2016

Product performance must be evaluated in a proper context. A concept & product test methodology provides it. (1-Aug-16)

The conclusions are only as good as the data they're based on. (8-Aug-16)

A questionnaire administered face-to-face by an interviewer must be designed differently from a self-completion one. (15-Aug-16)

Watch out for the order bias in the long list of responses when designing an offline pen-paper diary. (22-Aug-16)

In every research project, it's of the utmost importance to define very clearly in advance the expected outputs. (29-Aug-16)

September 2016

Beware of the few outspoken respondents representing only the minority in the actual population when conducting Qual Research. (5-Sep-16)

"Faster, cheaper, better" must be compensated by a very focused, short, and to-the-point questionnaire. (12-Sep-16)

In marketing research, the devil is also in the detail as well. (19-Sep-16)

Garbage in, garbage out. Fancy analysis and graphics can't cover up poorly executed field operations. (26-Sep-16)

October 2016

It's critical that the different panels in product testing projects are matched as closely as possible in all aspects. (3-Oct-16)

When designing a face-to-face interviewer administered questionnaire, try to put yourself in interviewers' shoes. (10-Oct-16)

In the restaurant business, ingredients determine the quality of the foods served. In MR, field quality is the key success factor. (17-Oct-16)

A better way to measure the length of interview in a survey is to count the number of questions. (24-Oct-16)

Each tool / technique has its own strengths and weaknesses. There's no perfect tool / technique. (31-Oct-16)

November 2016

Don't confuse research methodology with operations excellence. (7-Nov-16)

A quick reminder. Changing the methodology slightly might change the end results significantly. (14-Nov-16)

A tool should be selected not due to its sexiness but due to its ability to answer the research objective. (21-Nov-16)

We should wait for all data to be collected and tabulated before studying the summary statistics to get a more reliable estimate. This is a practical application of the Law of Large Numbers. (28-Nov-16)

December 2016

Research proposals are supposed to be evaluated comprehensively, not only the investment section. (5-Dec-16)

Questionnaire design & writing should really be left to professional marketing researchers. (12-Dec-16)

"If you don't have a point of difference, you'd better have a low price." (Jack Trout) (19-Dec-16)

In the end, comparing the quality of field service providers is like comparing SQ to Air Asia. (26-Dec-16)

2017

January 2017

Preventing a disease is much better than treating it. Conducting a concept product test must precede launching a new product. (1-Jan-17)

There're several variants of the implicit association research method. Beware of what you're buying from research agencies. (9-Jan-17)

Qualitative research asks "why" while quantitative research asks "what". (16-Jan-17)

In an unbranded product test, it's just too good to be true if respondents can guess the flavor or fragrance perfectly. (23-Jan-17)

Ignoring light and non-buyers of a brand is no recipe for growth (Byron Sharp). (30-Jan-17)

February 2017

Research objectives determine the data collection strategy, not the other way around. (6-Feb-17)

The huge amount & different types of data in your disposal are relevant only if they help you achieve your business objectives. (13-Feb-17)

It's a cardinal sin to tweak your data to fit your story. (20-Feb-17)

Every question in the questionnaire must have one and only one meaning. (27-Feb-17)

March 2017

It's a wishful thinking to expect fieldwork to be 100% efficient. Even machinery can't be 100% efficient. (6-Mar-17)

Even in data mining projects, the data in the customers database can still contain errors. (13-Mar-17)

Software package is only a tool to help you solve business problems. (20-Mar-17)

Churn is a good example where data mining and marketing research can complement each other. (27-Mar-17)

April 2017

Think of sample size as a magnifying glass. You need a bigger sample size to detect a smaller difference. (3-Apr-17)

Always focus on the research and business objectives when analyzing your data. (10-Apr-17)

Plan the analysis early, even at the proposal stage. Envision the end results as early as possible. (17-Apr-17)

Always prepare a proper table specs before you start your data analysis. (24-Apr-17)

May 2017

Once the data and tables from the Data Processing Department are ready, always check & recheck for errors. (1-May-17)

Sometimes, the best way to understand why customers did what they did is to ask them directly instead of trying to model it. (8-May-17)

Research agencies, don't ignore the intangible high mental cost dealing with poor operations when calculating your gross margin. (22-May-17)

The acceptance of a product should be based on the evaluation by common consumers, not an expert panel. (29-May-17)

June 2017

Calculating a rate card makes sense only if the specs are clearly defined & the variation from project to project is very small. (5-Jun-17)

R&D should also understand well the basics of marketing & marketing research to be able to support the business effectively. (12-Jun-17)

It's surprising that a test market is still being considered instead of a proper marketing research initiative in the 21st century. (19-Jun-17)

A customer experience survey must be conducted not too long from the actual event for customers to recall the experience well. (26-Jun-17)

July 2017

In an online survey, use a grid question sparingly since it actually counts as multiple questions. (3-Jul-17)

In an online or mobile survey, the layout of a grid question must be designed well to avoid confusing & tiring respondents. (10-Jul-17)

Business insight is only as good as the quality of data it's based on. (17-Jul-17)

Changing the layout and planogram of a store without any proper research could run the risk of alienating the loyal shoppers. (24-Jul-17)

You must not mislead respondents by providing a wrong description about your competitor's product in an unbranded product test. (31-Jul-17)

August 2017

Online or offline is only a data collection strategy. In the end, research objectives should dictate which one is better suited. (7-Aug-17)

Completing a 60-question mobile survey is an experience you don't want to repeat. (14-Aug-17)

Excellent fieldwork execution is a must in every marketing research projects, and also in Sea Games 2017. (21-Aug-17)

Marketing research can't perform witchcraft. You can't just ask respondents directly & then come up with a new positioning concept. (28-Aug-17)

September 2017

In a volumetric exercise, it's implicitly assumed that the concept & product are already optimized in the previous research stage. (4-Sep-17)

Big data project can be considered as providing the "inside view" while marketing research provides the "outside view". (11-Sep-17)

October 2017

Forcing customers to voice their opinion is not a good way to conduct a customer experience survey. (2-Oct-17)

Think of market research as your payment for relevant information to reduce risks in new product management. (9-Oct-17)

Cost Per Interview is a function of many factors; e.g., project type, sample size, respondent's criteria, no. of visits, interview length, and data collection method. (16-Oct-17)

To obtain the most cost-efficient proposal from a research agency, you must provide a concise specification including your detailed expected deliverables. (23-Oct-17)

A Usage & Attitude study is intended to capture a snapshot of the current market condition. (30-Oct-17)

November 2017

Behavioral economics covers a lot of topics; e.g., judgments, heuristics, biases, and choices. (6-Nov-17)

Marketing research can't guarantee any sales increase; probably only a price discount can. (13-Nov-17)

Variance of measurements from regular respondents can't be expected to be as low as that from trained panelists. (20-Nov-17)

In this digital age, it's unfortunate that some clients still consider doing a 3 to 4-hour usage & attitude study. (27-Nov-17)

December 2017

It's almost impossible to try to understand the market, the category, your brands, and users of your brands from just one marketing research project only. (4-Dec-17)

A "sexy" method should be selected because it can answer the business objectives well, not because of its "sexiness" only. (11-Dec-17)

Like Christmas which gives hope, market research casts light on the right direction businesses have to take. (25-Dec-17)

2018

January 2018

Newness of a methodology doesn't guarantee its validity and usefulness. Older methods have their own merits to be able to survive the test of time. (1-Jan-18)

When writing a survey questionnaire, avoid creating an imagery attribute in two sentences joined by the conjunction 'or'. (8-Jan-18)

Principles of behavioral economics can help designing a survey questionnaire which minimizes the inherent biases of respondents. They can also be used to nudge consumers to prefer your brands. (15-Jan-18)

Market research agencies can launch standard projects in a short time. Usually, it's the brand team who's having problem finalizing the stimulus in time. (22-Jan-18)

Faster, better, cheaper is a myth! (Robert G. Cooper, in Winning at New Products: Creating Value Through Innovation, 5th Ed., 2017) (29-Jan-18)

February 2018

To date, 2017 was the peak of the marketing research business in Indonesia. Hopefully the positive trend would continue in 2018, the "election year" (*Tahun Pilkada*). (5-Feb-18)

Is there any correlation between the involvement of Procurement and the decline in the quality in the marketing research world? (12-Feb-18)

When you're creating a new product or service and want to test it on your prospects, make sure you set aside a big enough budget to finance the research. (19-Feb-18)

When business is good, you don't value research and data. When business is poor, you suddenly realize that you've got no data to guide you in the right direction. (26-Feb-18)

March 2018

Brand managers should have a mastery of marketing research principles to be able to write a proper research brief. (5-Mar-18)

If a research project is unplanned and there is only a limited budget, don't expect a comprehensive research design. (12-Mar-18)

Without explicitly written criteria in the research brief, no marketing research agency can prepare a complete questionnaire. (19-Mar-18)

When testing your new product in a marketing research project, make sure you benchmark it against an existing product in the same class. (26-Mar-18)

April 2018

Marketing research should be indispensable in an "evidence-based decision making" process. (2-Apr-18)

An "evidence-based decision making" process must start with a clearly defined business objective. (9-Apr-18)

An "evidence-based decision making" process would rely on the solid data sensemaking skills of the analysts to be able to be completed successfully. (16-Apr-18)

An "evidence-based decision making" process should be augmented by good technologies to run smoothly and efficiently. (23-Apr-18)

A boutique research agency doesn't mean a cheap research agency. (30-Apr-18)

May 2018

In this environmentally friendly era, it's just a shame to demand research agencies to submit a hard copy of the proposal. (7-May-18)

It's just an overkill to invite 6 research agencies to pitch for a standard concept-product test project. (14-May-18)

Brand Managers, research will be just a waste of valuable resources if you, yourselves, are not sure what you're trying to sell to consumers. (21-May-18)

Qualitative research results in general are not supposed to be generalized to the wider population. (28-May-18)

June 2018

"It is worth repeating the truism that research methods should be chosen based on the specific task at hand." (in Doing Qualitative Research by David Silverman, 5th Ed., 2018) (4-Jun-18)

When developing close-ended questions in your questionnaire, make sure to include "Not Applicable" as one of the possible answers. (11-Jun-18)

In the self-completion mode of data collection, each question must be very precise without any double interpretation. (18-Jun-18)

Without access to retail audit and consumer panel data, it's just extremely difficult to monitor the market movement and develop the appropriate growth strategy for the brand. (25-Jun-18)

July 2018

Qualitative researchers must also understand the principles of experimentation like randomization and rotation to minimize bias. (2-Jul-18)

Fieldwork cost can be reduced by hiring inexperienced interviewers and letting go the proper field training and the various standard quality control checks at the expense of quality. (9-Jul-18)

A census will collect information from all relevant participants in the population, not just from a subset of the population. (16-Jul-18)

Marketing research can only provide a prediction via a simulation. The actual results must be confirmed via an experimentation. (23-Jul-18)

Before conducting a post launch check, you need to wait and give enough time to the consumers to be aware of your brand and buy it. (30-Jul-18)

August 2018

Technology still can't replace basic marketing research skills like designing and writing a good questionnaire. (6-Aug-18)

The proliferation of small research agencies, originated from fieldwork suppliers, with only barely minimum technical competencies but offering a full marketing research service might deteriorate the quality of research in general. (13-Aug-18)

When commissioning a large scale quantitative project to a fieldwork supplier directly, make sure your supplier has a strong enough financial resource to be able to complete the project. (20-Aug-18)

When doing data collection via an online or mobile panel, you need to let go imposing various quotas on your sample to be able to complete fieldwork within a reasonable time frame unless your panel database is extremely huge. (27-Aug-18)

September 2018

A new method takes time to create, develop, evaluate, test in a real situation, and implement commercially. (3-Sep-18)

Marketing is not an exact science. A proper scientific experiment, if possible, would help supporting or refuting a marketing theory. (10-Sep-18)

It's just unfortunate when research is used only to support an argument in an internal political debate within a company. (17-Sep-18)

When you've got a predetermined bias favoring a particular research method, you just can't see that another research method would be more suitable to achieve your objectives. (24-Sep-18)

October 2018

Small businesses can conduct a simple market research just by interviewing their own employees who may already know customers' likes, dislikes, and preferences. (1-Oct-18)

When your Discussion Guide covers everything from A to Z, it indicates that you have no clue what you want to get out of the research and you are just on a big fishing expedition. (8-Oct-18)

It must be made a standard operating procedure that the R&D team must attend every product testing marketing research presentation. (15-Oct-18)

In a self-completion mode of data collection, researchers should from time to time try out the questionnaires themselves to empathize with the respondents. (22-Oct-18)

Consumers are not brand managers. It doesn't make sense to expect them to think like a brand manager in a survey or focus group. (29-Oct-18)

November 2018

You must really think way out of the box to design a brand health check study covering 4 different categories in 7 different cities with a budget of only IDR 100 million. (5-Nov-18)

It's just a waste of resource when clients rush you for a proposal but at the end the initiative gets postponed indefinitely since the brand team can't produce the stimulus. (12-Nov-18)

A CEO should understand well and fully what marketing research is all about before condemning it useless. (19-Nov-18)

A good research would provide a guidance in your company intentional growth plan. (26-Nov-18)

December 2018

Software and tools can't replace the skills possessed by a well trained Statistician. (3-Dec-18)

A mobile panel can provide a quick, simple, and cheap solution to screen out non-critical options. (10-Dec-18)

Having more participants in one focus group discussion doesn't necessarily yield better insights. (17-Dec-18)

Qualitative research is useful in an exploratory study since the moderator has the flexibility to change the flow of questioning and the questions during a focus group discussion. (24-Dec-18)

A New Year wish: leave managing research to the research professionals. (31-Dec-18)

2019

January 2019

Data collection strategy depends strongly on the research objectives and project constraints like time and cost. (7-Jan-19)

A poorly designed research is worse than no research at all. (14-Jan-19)

No matter how big or small your data are, the appropriate research design and methodology will always depend on your objectives. (21-Jan-19)

A good researcher must act as a trusted advisor for the client, not as a slave. (28-Jan-19)

February 2019

Very small businesses can also benefit from market research by asking for a simple feedback from their customers before launching a new promotion. (4-Feb-19)

A little knowledge is indeed dangerous. However, it's even more dangerous if you ignore experts' advice. (11-Feb-19)

It's surprising that some researchers still don't understand that different data collection methods could yield different results. (18-Feb-19)

It's just insane if you choose a particular software tool to boast only. (25-Feb-19)

March 2019

Marketers who don't fully understand their own business issues can't write accurate research briefs. (4-Mar-19)

To be able to extract some consumer insights for decision making purposes, you need to conduct some research. Doing a consumer research does require some investment. (11-Mar-19)

It's just discouraging that some business folks still don't understand that marketing research must go through a proper process to extract good insights from the respondents. (18-Mar-19)

In a quantitative research, diagnostics would cause the questionnaire to be longer and the project cost to increase due to the additional analyses incurred. (25-Mar-19)

April 2019

Quantitative research tries hard to shorten the length of interview to under 30 minutes while a focus group discussion can easily last for 3 hours. (1-Apr-19)

Conducting a proper product testing project takes time since we need to give enough time to the consumers we've recruited as respondents to experience the product and form their opinion. (8-Apr-19)

All people involved in the business of consumer insights must really master the fundamental of marketing research. (15-Apr-19)

It's just discouraging that some researchers still don't get it that the results you obtain from conducting the same marketing research project in different countries could be different. (22-Apr-19)

Consultants are needed to assist and guide busy marketers to implement the latest findings from science to improve business results. (29-Apr-19)

About the Author

T.S. Lim is currently a Quantitative Senior Research Director & Partner at Leap Research (http://leap-research.com).

He has more than 18 years experiences in the marketing research industry. He's held senior positions with the global marketing research agencies Research International Indonesia and Ipsos Indonesia. He's a seasoned marketing researcher in the innovation related projects; e.g., concept screening and testing, product testing, concept & product testing, and packaging testing. He's also very familiar with brand equity research as well as market understanding.

He's a Statistician by training with a Bachelor degree in Mathematics from the University of Indonesia and a Master of Science degree in Statistics from the University of Wisconsin-Madison, USA, where he has also completed PhD level courses in Statistics. He's a member of ESOMAR (http://bit.ly/tslim_esomar).

www.ingramcontent.com/pod-product-compliance
Lightning Source LLC
Chambersburg PA
CBHW081025170526
45158CB00010B/3155